To: Roger Springfield
"Hardest Worker"
Mooredale Jr. Club
1974

FROM: Michael
          Bar

SPORTS ILLUSTRATED
BOOK OF SMALL BOAT SAILING

SPORTS ILLUSTRATED

Book of

SMALL BOAT SAILING

BY THE EDITORS OF SPORTS ILLUSTRATED

J. B. LIPPINCOTT COMPANY
Philadelphia and New York
1960

COPYRIGHT © 1955, 1958, 1959 BY TIME INC.
PRINTED IN THE UNITED STATES OF AMERICA
LIBRARY OF CONGRESS CATALOG CARD NUMBER: 60-7843
FIFTH PRINTING

CONTENTS

CONTENTS

SPORTS ILLUSTRATED
BOOK OF SMALL BOAT SAILING

A Lightning, Typical of the Class Boats, Going to Windward

1

CLASS BOATS

THE LANGUAGE
OF SAILING

The landlubber who goes aboard a small boat will quickly find himself exposed to a foreign language. Class boat sailing has a sizeable vocabulary which is constantly in use by sailors.

In order to prepare you for the nautical words and phrases which will be used on the following pages, we have included not only a list of sailors' terms, but also a diagram showing the various points of sailing and an illustration clearly showing details of a Snipe, a representative small boat, its sails, rigging, and hull.

1

A GLOSSARY
OF NAUTICAL JARGON

BOW: front of boat

STERN: rear end of boat

ABEAM: straight out from side of boat

QUARTER: side of boat near the stern

AFT: toward the stern, or behind it

FORWARD: toward the bow

TOPSIDES: sides of the boat from the water-line to the deck

MAST: vertical pole supporting sails

BOOM: horizontal pole along bottom of sail

STAYS: wires from mast to deck, for support of mast

LINE: general term for rope

HALYARD: line used for raising or lowering a sail

SHEET: line used in adjusting the angle of a sail to the wind

BLOCK: sailors' term for pulley

TRIM: to adjust angle of sails to wind

LUFFING: shaking of sails that occurs when boat heads too much into the wind or sail is improperly trimmed

TO REEF: to lessen a sail's area by gathering in and tying down part of the sail

POINTING: sailing as close into the wind as possible

RUNNING: sailing with the wind more or less astern

BEARING OFF: steering more to leeward, or away from the wind

HEADING UP: steering more to windward, or towards the wind

BLANKETING: when windward boat takes wind from leeward boat's sails

BACKWINDING: when one sail throws wind onto lee side of another sail

HEELING: when a boat leans over

KNOT: one nautical mile (6,080 feet) per hour

2

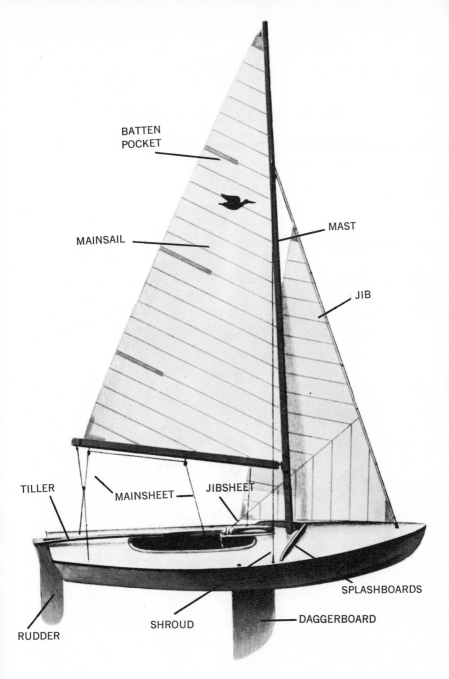

BATTEN POCKET

MAINSAIL

MAST

JIB

TILLER

MAINSHEET

JIBSHEET

SPLASHBOARDS

RUDDER

SHROUD

DAGGERBOARD

3

POINTS OF SAILING

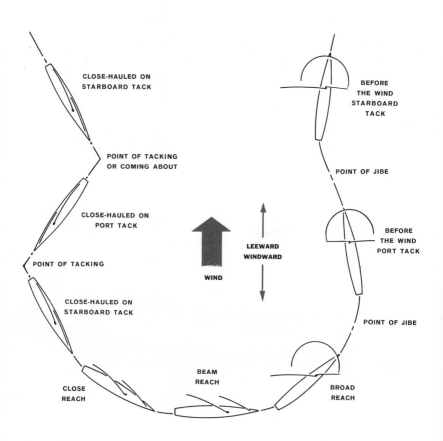

CLOSE-HAULED ON
STARBOARD TACK

BEFORE
THE WIND
STARBOARD
TACK

POINT OF TACKING
OR COMING ABOUT

POINT OF JIBE

CLOSE-HAULED ON
PORT TACK

LEEWARD
WINDWARD

BEFORE
THE WIND
PORT TACK

POINT OF TACKING

WIND

CLOSE-HAULED ON
STARBOARD TACK

POINT OF JIBE

BEAM
REACH

CLOSE
REACH

BROAD
REACH

Though a sailboat can sail a straight line away from the wind, or to **leeward**, it cannot go directly upwind **(windward, or to weather)**. Therefore, it zigzags, or **tacks** (*opposite*), as close as possible to the direction from which the wind is blowing, changing direction each time so that the windward side becomes the leeward side. When moving in this manner, the boat is **beating, close-hauled,** or **on the wind;** and when the wind is coming over the right **(starboard)** side, the boat is on the **starboard tack.** When the wind is coming from the left **(port)** side, the boat is on the **port tack.** A boat in the act of tacking to windward is **coming about** or **going about.** A boat in the act of tacking downwind is **jibing.** A boat can be on port or starboard tack whether it is beating, sailing a little farther away from the wind on a **close reach,** straight across the wind on a **beam reach,** still farther away from the wind on a **broad reach** or in the same direction as the wind, **before the wind.**

SMALL BOATS:
A REPRESENTATIVE SAMPLING

Here is an illustrated gallery of some of the most popular class boats in the United States, accompanied by details of their size, price, and sailing characteristics.

LIGHTNING

with over 8,000 in class, is one of the more popular sailboats in U.S. She is 19 feet long, ideal for racing, loafing; is in the upper medium price range.

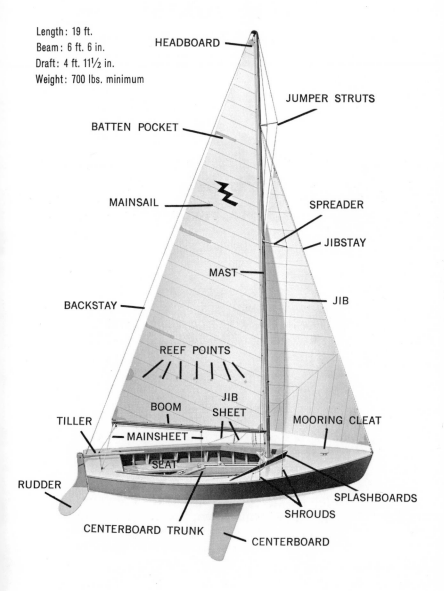

Length: 19 ft.
Beam: 6 ft. 6 in.
Draft: 4 ft. 11½ in.
Weight: 700 lbs. minimum

HEADBOARD

JUMPER STRUTS

BATTEN POCKET

MAINSAIL

SPREADER

JIBSTAY

MAST

JIB

BACKSTAY

REEF POINTS

JIB
SHEET

BOOM

TILLER

MOORING CLEAT

MAINSHEET

SEAT

RUDDER

SPLASHBOARDS

SHROUDS

CENTERBOARD TRUNK

CENTERBOARD

7

FLYING
DUTCHMAN

One of the most fascinating of the new planing hulls is the Flying Dutchman, a European design only three years old yet numbering more than 400 boats. The Dutchman has a clean, ribless plywood or fiber glass construction, and will hit speeds of 15 mph or more when she rises out of water and planes. Her cockpit provides racing quarters for two men or wide-open comfort for a five- or six-man pleasure sail. Included in the racing rig is a wild-looking trapeze, a belt and wire arrangement slung from up the mast, which makes it possible for the crewman to dangle far out to windward, doubling his efficiency for keeping the boat on an even keel where she sails the fastest.

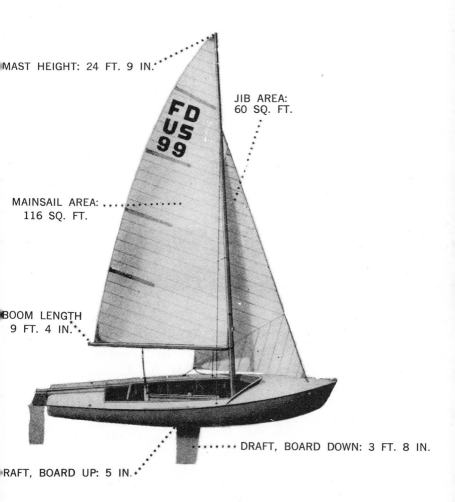

MAST HEIGHT: 24 FT. 9 IN.

JIB AREA:
60 SQ. FT.

MAINSAIL AREA:
116 SQ. FT.

BOOM LENGTH
9 FT. 4 IN.

DRAFT, BOARD DOWN: 3 FT. 8 IN.

RAFT, BOARD UP: 5 IN.

Length: 19 ft. 10 in.
Beam: 5 ft. 7 in.
Designer: U. van Essen,
    Bussum, Holland

Working sails: mainsail, jib
Racing sails: genoa, spinnaker
Weight: 374 lbs.
Low priced

9

THE SNIPE

A trim 15 feet 6 inches over-all, with a 5-foot beam and 20-foot 3-inch mast, the Snipe draws 40 inches with daggerboard down, has two sails, main and jib, and a measured sail area (up to 115 square feet) which makes her an easy boat to handle. For racing she takes a skipper and one crew. Costs range from very inexpensive kits, to modestly priced ready-to-sail. Outfitted for racing, the Snipe costs a bit more. There have been 12,000 registered since 1931, and 4,000 are now active.

PELICAN

The Pelican (*right*) is the godchild of the boating widows of Miami whose husbands left them sitting on the dock during the weekend. Fed up with spending their time ashore, the women shopped around for a small, simple boat for themselves. Harold Glander, South Miami boat builder, responded with the Pelican. Small and light, with a minimum of running gear, the Pelican is as easy to handle as any boat afloat. She races well with two aboard, but is beamy enough to hold four adults for an afternoon sail. Her speed in a breeze is about four knots, and in heavy winds she can skim along at better than five. Best of all, with her fat, flat-ended design, she can stand up in winds over 30 knots. The ladies, however, are still having trouble. On more than one weekend, the husbands have deserted their big boats to race in the sporty Pelicans, leaving the wives once again on the dock.

Length: 11 ft. 2 in.
Beam: 4 ft. 7 in.
Weight: 140 lbs.
Price: under $1,000.
Designer: Harold Glander,
    South Miami, Fla.

MAST HEIGHT:
17 FT. 6 IN.

MAINSAIL AREA: 62 SQ. FT.

BOOM LENGTH:
8 FT. 6 IN.

DRAFT: 6 IN.

DRAFT, BOARD DOWN: 2 FT. 6 IN.

13

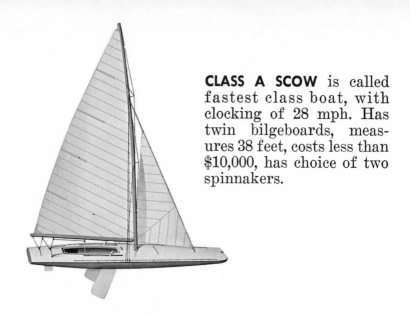

CLASS A SCOW is called fastest class boat, with clocking of 28 mph. Has twin bilgeboards, measures 38 feet, costs less than $10,000, has choice of two spinnakers.

Y-FLYER has many fleets in Midwest and in Canada, is baby cousin of Class A Scow. She is 18 feet overall, is in the low-priced field, counts about 500 boats in fast-growing class.

14

THISTLE, with new gadgets like halyard winches built into mast and roller reefing drum on boom, is one of fastest-growing classes, now counts 1250. The price is low to medium.

BEETLE CAT has ungainly gaff-headed rig, but is safe, broad-beamed all-weather boat. A handy boat in shallow waters, she measures 12 feet 4 inches, costs about $1,000. The class has 1800 boats.

15

PENGUIN is tiny, 11½-foot centerboarder adapted to shallow bays and ponds. About 5,000 are scattered around country. Low-priced, Penguins are perfect for children.

WOOD PUSSY is cat-rigged centerboard boat measuring 13 feet 6 inches over-all. Wood Pussy costs about $1,000; its racing activity is concentrated in Northeast.

COMET is excellent boat in light air. There are over 4,000 boats in the class. In the low medium price range, she is 16 feet long, has cockpit big enough to hold two sailors.

CHALLENGER MOTH measures 11 feet, is subdivision of over-all Moth Class which has many modifications. The total class registration is 4,000. Price for new Moth: less than $1,000.

17

INTERNATIONAL 14 claims to be fastest sailboat of her size (14 feet). With spinnaker set, she'll plane at 14 knots. Medium priced, she is best in steady breeze.

INTERNATIONAL 110 is sleek, 24-foot double-ender that pivots very easily on her hook-shaped keel. She carries a spinnaker, and is in the lower-medium price range. There are about 650 of this class in the United States.

STAR measures 22 feet 8½ inches, is truly international racer (4,000 entries on five continents). She is medium priced, is hauled out, kept bone-dry between races.

RAVEN is fast, 24-foot centerboarder. Popular in New England and Long Island (class now totals 300), she is upper-medium priced, has pioneered in using fiber glass for hull.

INTERNATIONAL ONE-DE-SIGN is 33 feet 2 inches long, handles beautifully in heavy weather. International sells for $9,500 with sails. There are 130 International One-Designs in the United States.

DRAGON is favorite boat of Queen Elizabeth and Duke of Edinburgh. Dragon carries spinnaker and genoa, has cabin with room enough for two. Sells well in excess of $4,000. Of 2,000-odd boats, about 160 are in the United States.

2

SAILING TO WINDWARD

For most of the million or more small-boat sailors in the United States, the Lightning typifies the many kinds of standard hulls known as class boats, whose fleets are the backbone of the nation's sailing. A boat like the Lightning offers the average yachtsman fast competition and safe fun in one tight package. Furthermore, it is the perfect training vehicle—simple in rig, easy to sail, lively and powerful in a breeze. In this section Bill Cox of the Noroton, Conn., Yacht Club, twice International Lightning Champion and a top racing skipper for 35 years, sets forth techniques of rigging and sailing that will be helpful to any class boat owner, beginner or expert.——THE EDITORS

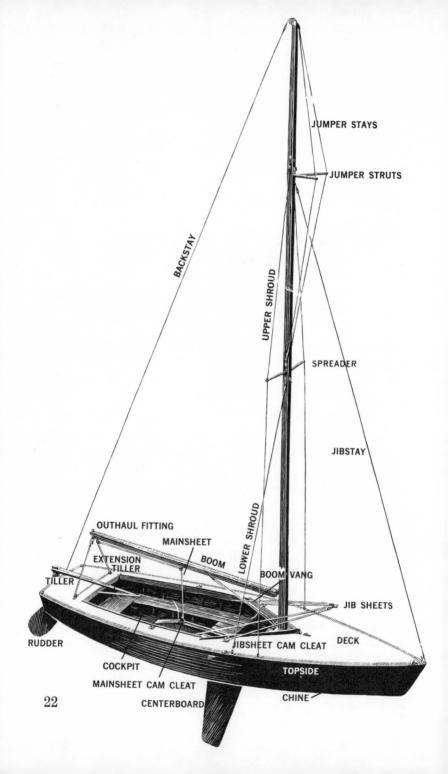

JUMPER STAYS

JUMPER STRUTS

BACKSTAY

UPPER SHROUD

SPREADER

JIBSTAY

LOWER SHROUD

OUTHAUL FITTING

MAINSHEET

BOOM

EXTENSION
TILLER

BOOM VANG

TILLER

JIB SHEETS

RUDDER

JIBSHEET CAM CLEAT

DECK

COCKPIT

MAINSHEET CAM CLEAT

TOPSIDE

CENTERBOARD

CHINE

22

NO. 1 FAMILY RACING CLASS

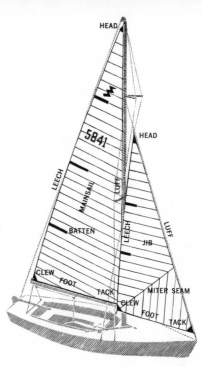

More families race the 19-foot Lightning than any other type of sailboat. There are more than 8,000 of these versatile craft, 3,500 of which are owned and raced by members of the Lightning Class Association, one of the largest organized groups of active racers anywhere. The outstanding features of the Lightning, essentially unchanged since Olin Stephens first designed it in 1938, are her stable, roomy hull (*left*), her well-balanced sail plan (*above*), which includes a large spinnaker—not shown here but to be discussed in detail in Section 3. Moreover, she is in the medium price range ready to sail, and there is a lively secondhand market from coast to coast. Finally, she has a retractable centerboard, as opposed to a fixed keel, so she can easily be hauled from place to place on a trailer or stored in the garage for the winter. Best of all, she can be eased off a mud bank or sand bar if the skipper suffers a lapse in navigation.

24

TUNING THE MAST

First problem with Lightning or any other small boat of similar rig is to place mast in approximate position for proper boat balance and to ensure that it will remain straight under the strain of sailing. Recommended sequence of steps below begins with tuning ashore, in which the jumper stays are set up. Next comes tuning at mooring and tuning under way. Then come the refinements of combination tuning, which is purely trial and error and may take considerable time, since adjustment in one stay often means compensating adjustments in other stays.

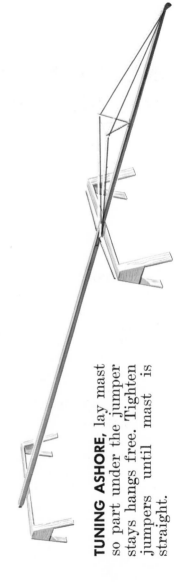

TUNING ASHORE, lay mast so part under the jumper stays hangs free. Tighten jumpers until mast is straight.

TUNING AT MOORING, start with all stays slack, then tighten upper shrouds (*below left, in blue*) so mast has equal clearance on each side of deck opening. Next adjust jibstay and backstay (*below right, in blue*). Begin by moving butt of mast and setting jibstay so that mast just touches rear edge of deck opening when top of mast has 10 to 15 inches of rake (backward lean). Now tighten backstay till masthead begins bending back, then loosen backstay until mast is straight. Place wooden wedges at foot of mast and in forward part of deck opening.

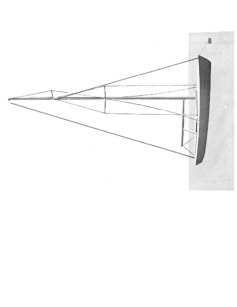

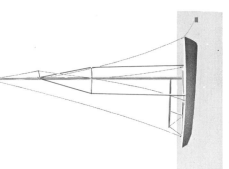

25

TUNING UNDER WAY begins with both lower shrouds (*below, in blue*) hanging slightly slack. On starboard tack (*left*) sight up rear of mast, which will probably be curved left or right. Pull inward on starboard lower shroud. If the mast straightens, the lower shroud needs tightening. If bend increases, pull inward on upper starboard shroud. If the mast now straightens, lower shroud needs loosening. Use same procedure to tune mast on port tack (*right*) by adjusting lower port shroud. Repeat entire procedure until mast is straight on both tacks.

COMBINATION TUNING removes any remaining bends in the mast and puts as much tension as possible on jibstay so that jib will hold its proper shape. Use the backstay, jumpers and the lower shrouds only (*all in blue*). There is no set sequence. Start on one tack and straighten most obvious bends first, working around to minor bends. Then go onto the opposite tack and do the same. Return to mooring, use deck ladder to reach the jumpers for any needed adjustments in the upper mast section. Repeat cycle until jibstay is taut and mast stands straight on both tacks.

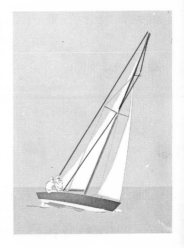

TUNING ERRORS resulting in forward or backward bowing of mast (*in blue*) will reduce effectiveness of mainsail, designed for straight mast. With jibstay and upper shrouds taut, point on mast at top of jibstay (*blue dot*) is held in fixed position relative to hull. When masthead bends back, mast below blue dot bulges forward. Correct by loosening backstay, tightening jumpers and lower shrouds. When masthead bends forward, mast below the dot bulges backward. Backstay must be tightened and lower shrouds, jumpers loosened. Never correct forward or backward bend with jibstay or upper shrouds.

27

CONTROLLING
THE ANGLE OF HEEL

The degree to which a boat heels, or tilts,
determines the shape of its hull under
water. Since the most desirable underwater shape depends on speed of boat,
the crew must shift weight when speed
changes. In light wind when speed is
low, resistance of hull comes from friction between hull and water. To reduce
resistance, area of hull under water is
reduced by making boat heel inten-
tionally (*upper left, page 30*). At medium speed, best shape results when the
windward chine (where bottom joins
topsides) is about two inches out of
water (*page 31*). At high speed in strong
winds, greatest resistance results because boat makes waves. Keeping boat
as level as possible (*opposite*) reduces
wave formation and thus resistance.
Arrows indicate wind direction.

HEAVY BREEZE brings the crew out on the windward deck to hike, or lean out over water. In hard puffs (*below*) skipper hikes also, purposely spilling wind out of the mainsail to keep the boat from tipping over too far.

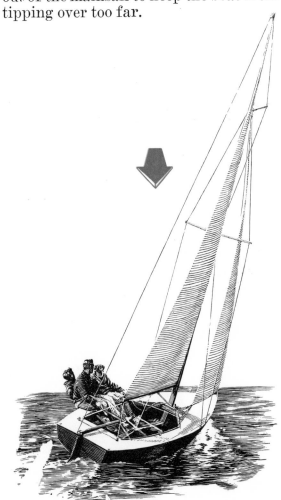

LIGHT BREEZE calls for the crew to sit on the leeward deck (*upper left*) and to make boat heel over as much as possible. Skipper makes use of extension tiller so he too can get his weight well to leeward.

MEDIUM BREEZE finds the crew on windward side of the cockpit (*large illustration*), or divided between sides of boat, keeping windward chine two inches off the water. Skipper sits to windward whenever possible.

GOING AGAINST THE WIND

No boat can sail directly into the wind (*see arrow*), since sails will not fill. However, a boat can arrive at a point directly upwind by making a series of diagonal slants, or tacks, first one way, then another (*upper left, page 34*). Sequence opposite shows proper way to make boat come about, that is, go from one tack to another. Skipper starts by pushing tiller to leeward. As boat turns into wind, crewman lets jib sheet go, and mainsail starts to move across the cockpit. Critical moment comes when boat is headed directly into wind (*middle illustration*). Wind no longer fills sails. However, if maneuver is carried out smoothly, momentum of turn will carry boat over onto opposite tack. In third illustration, boat has moved successfully onto new tack. Crew has fastened jib on lee side in position to form important aerodynamic wind slot (*see pages 36-37*) between jib and mainsail.

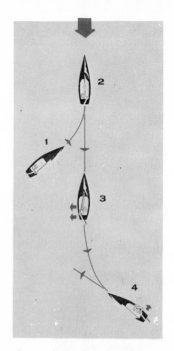

UPWIND SAILING is done in series of tacks made at 45° angle to wind (*above, left*). This is as close to wind direction as boats can sail effectively. Surface ripples show direction of wind on water, or true wind. On moving hull, true wind is altered by forward speed of boat. This produces slightly different wind direction, called apparent wind. It lies between true wind and bow and is force that actually drives hull. **UPWIND CRISIS** occurs when boat (1) tries to come about but fails to complete maneuver. Boat loses forward speed, stops (2), finally drifts backward out of control. This is called "getting in irons." To get out of irons, skipper pushes tiller and boom away from himself and holds them there (3). The stern soon swings to one side, mainsail fills and boat stops moving backward. At that point skipper pulls tiller toward him (4) and boat gains headway on new tack. Maneuver can be hastened when crew holds jib to side opposite the mainsail.

34

POWER FROM SAILS

When a boat is tacking upwind, two distinct forces combine to drive it ahead. First, as wind strikes windward side of sail and is deflected along its curve, wind exerts pressure on sail and, because sail is curved, part of this pressure acts in a forward direction to drive the boat ahead. The remaining pressure acts to push the boat sidewise, but this tendency is virtually nullified by centerboard, so that sidewise pressure is actually converted into heeling. Second, wind which slips along the lee side of sail travels faster than wind on the windward side. Therefore a relative low-pressure area forms on lee side which tends to suck the sail ahead, and with it the boat. This aerodynamic force actually provides more than twice as much forward drive as pressure on windward side. On a boat with a jib, this force is very powerfully augmented by presence of the slot effect (*next page*). Resultant drive from all these sources makes sailboat able to go faster diagonally into wind than it will go downwind. In addition, proper set and shape of sails (*page 38*) is vital in order to get most driving power out of any given amount of wind filling the sails.

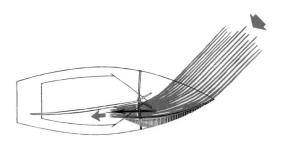

SLOT EFFECT occurs when jib funnels air through slot formed between jib and mainsail (*see arrow in drawing at left and overhead view of slot above*). Narrowness of slot forces air to increase speed. This causes strong low-pressure area on lee side of mainsail (by operation of Bernoulli's principle, any increase in airflow speed decreases internal pressure of the air at that point). This "vacuum" pulls boat ahead and is by far most important factor in sail power.

ADJUSTING SLOT by varying jib's distance from the mainsail is done by tightening or loosening jib sheet. Bringing the jib too close (*below, left*) causes wind to deflect into the mainsail. Mainsail then curves away from jib. Slot becomes distorted and loses its effectiveness. Correct jib position (*below, right*) smoothly funnels wind parallel to lee side of mainsail. Jib should set slightly closer to mainsail in strong wind than in light. In racing, changing length of jib sheet by two inches or so can well make the difference between winning and losing.

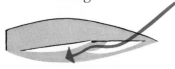

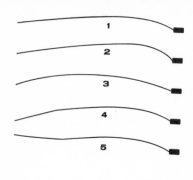

SAIL SHAPES can either help or hinder smooth flow of air along surfaces of sail. Diagram at left shows five common shapes of mainsails. From top, most desirable shape (1) is curve which flattens more and more toward leech. Sail with too much curve forward (2) is too easily backwinded by jib. Uniform curve (3), mistakenly shunned by many, is good in light wind. Sail with tight leech (4) is bad in strong wind, while loose leech (5) is poor shape in any wind.

SHAPING MAINSAIL will help increase power. For strong winds, flatten sail by pulling on downhaul and outhaul (*blue line, left below, indicates flattened curve*). For light winds, get a fuller curve by slacking off on outhaul and downhaul (*blue line, right below, indicates deepened curve*).

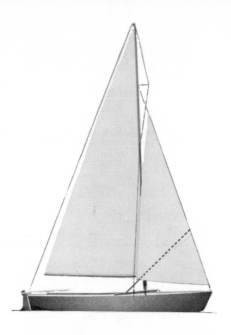

SHAPING JIB for greatest power, primary consideration is that jibstay remain very taut. Second factor is the proper location of jib-sheet leads on deck. In Lightning, correctly placed jib leads will hold jib so that line of sight (*see dotted line, top diagram*) up jib sheet (or halfway between double sheets) will cross jib luff about eight inches above miter seam. Viewed from above (*bottom diagram*), sheets extended through leads to bow should form angle of 13° or less with centerline of hull. If the leads are set correctly, entire length of jib luff will flutter at the same time when boat swings into the wind.

SHAPING SAIL

SHAPING WITH SHEET, the skipper should try to get a direct downpull on leech of mainsail to bring it into plane formed by mast and boom. Standard mainsheet rig on Lightnings (*below, left*) does this better than optional bridle rig used by many Lightnings (*below, right*). Bridle rig lets leech of mainsail sag off (*below, right, in blue*), whereas sail trimmed with standard rig can be pushed to leeward by hand, where friction in mainsheet blocks will hold boom out so one strand of mainsheet gets direct downpull.

SHAPING WITH BOOM VANG is best way to keep mainsail leech straight during strong, puffy winds when mainsheet has to be slacked quickly from time to time to spill wind. Otherwise, boom vang (*p. 41, blue*) is seldom used in windward sailing, since downward pull of mainsheet will keep leech straight enough. However, on courses across the wind and downwind, boom vang should be in constant use to keep leech straight and boom under control, since, on these points of sailing, the boom hangs farther out and mainsheet cannot pull hard enough to control boom.

40

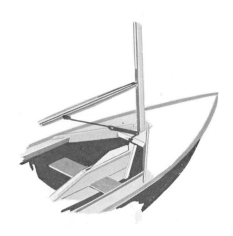

BALANCE OF BOAT

When all wind and water forces affecting a sailboat are in proper balance and boat is sailed at 45° angle to true wind with tiller held at dead center (*page 43*), the hull will travel forward in a straight line. If tiller must be held to windward to keep boat on a straight course at 45° angle to wind (*page 42, right*), boat has weather helm; if tiller must be held to leeward (*top, page 42*), boat has lee helm. Boat with lee or weather helm is slowed down because of continual drag of rudder, which must be held at angle to keep boat on course. In a race, weather helm should be corrected immediately (*page 44*) or boat will soon be passed by others. Lee helm is serious for even non-competitive sailors because boat will be reluctant to head up safely in strong puff. Although in properly balanced boat rudder is amidships when boat sail˜ straight course, rudder should transmit slight leeward pull to tiller. This shows rudder is helping centerboard resist leeward drift. When tiller does not have leeward pull and feels dead in skipper's hand, this means boat is not properly balanced, and correction as if for a slight leeward helm should be made (*page 48*).

LEE HELM occurs in a boat that heads away from wind when the tiller is held amidships. To stay on course, tiller must be put to leeward.

WEATHER HELM occurs in a boat that tends to head into wind when the tiller is held amidships, so tiller has to be held to windward.

PROPER HELM keeps boat on course with rudder amidships. Ideally, there should be slight pressure wanting to swing the tiller to leeward.

CORRECTING WEATHER HELM

In heavy weather, all conventional sailing craft create a large leeward bow wave which pushes bow to windward and causes a temporary weather helm. One way to correct this temporary weather helm is to move crew back in cockpit (*above*), bringing forward part of boat out of water (*see arrows above*) and reducing bow wave. Do not use this technique in milder weather to correct weather helm but apply remedies for permanent weather helm which follow. First remedy for permanent weather helm is to lift centerboard a few inches (*bottom of diagram opposite*). Most effective remedy of all is to reduce rake of mast (*opposite*), then retune entire rig. On following pages are five other cures.

CORRECTING BY BALANCING, keep boat as level as possible, since level boat makes smaller leeward bow wave. By keeping boat on even keel, you will also bring center of effort (point in sail plan where force of wind is theoretically concentrated) more nearly over center of lateral resistance (point under hull where total force resisting drift is theoretically located). This means less weather helm.

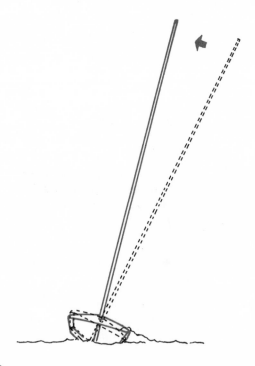

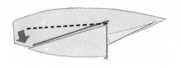 

CORRECTING BY TRIMMING can be accomplished by easing mainsheet or trimming jib sheets—or both. Even though these adjustments may interfere with best setting of sails at given moment, boat will, nevertheless, perform better, since weather helm causes greater loss of speed than badly trimmed sails. In a heavy wind, easing mainsheet gives far better results than trimming jib.

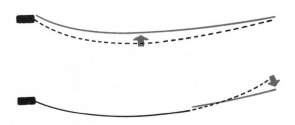

CORRECTING BY SHAPING mainsail can be done simply by flattening curve of mainsail (*upper, above*). Tight leech may also cause weather helm. Stretching leech by hand may produce flatter curve aft (*lower, above*). However, leech tight enough to cause a permanent weather helm will probably have to be resewn by a sailmaker.

47

CORRECTING
LEE HELM

Since lee helm is opposite to weather helm in every respect, corrective measures are opposite. Preferred method is to increase rake in mast and then retune the rig Other remedies for lee helm are to move crew forward, ease jib sheet, pull in mainsail, make mainsail take fuller curve by slacking outhaul and downhaul, or lo er centerboard. For maximum centerboard correction, top edges of centerboard trunk can be notched to let centerboard swing as far forward as class rules will allow. Lee helm in moderate and heavy conditions is particularly dangerous because boat bears off in hard puffs when, for safety's sake, skipper is trying to head boat into wind to spill wind from sails. Problem is particularly acute with centerboard boats, which lack stability afforded by heavy ballast of metal keel.

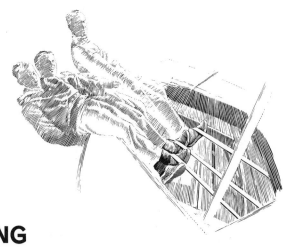

HIKING
TO WINDWARD

The most strenuous and exciting moment in class boat sailing comes when a sudden puff strikes, heeling boat so more of bottom than usual comes out of water (*next page*). To counteract sudden heeling, crew immediately hikes, hanging almost entirely out of boat, held in only by hiking straps (*above*). Skipper does his part in hiking, at same time steering with very end of extension tiller to head boat into wind (*next page*). He eases mainsheet to spill some of wind safely out of mainsail. In hiking, all hands should move quickly, since every second saved in bringing boat back to proper sailing angle means gaining on competitors, as well as safer and more comfortable sailing position. Peaks of action like this make sailing men love the sport.

HIKING WAY OUT
TO WINDWARD

3

SAILING TO LEEWARD

In this section Champion Bill Cox discusses the question of getting downwind with maximum speed. Primarily, this means sailing much of the time with a spinnaker billowing out over the bow. It also means extra watchfulness by the crew. The spinnaker is a tricky, powerful sail that must be handled with respect. But it can also be a lot of fun. Properly set in a good wind, the spinnaker can provide the most exciting ride of the day. However, proper setting requires skill, coordination and fast action. On the following pages the two most difficult maneuvers with a spinnaker—setting and jibing—are described step by step.——THE EDITORS

SETTING THE SPINNAKER

The spinnaker is not fastened along one of its edges to a stay or to the mast as are other sails. Instead, it floats free in the breeze, a spherical triangle held only at the corners. The head or upper corner is held aloft by the spinnaker halyard, which serves to raise the spinnaker. The tack (lower corner next to the spinnaker pole) is attached to one end of the spinnaker guy. The clew (the other lower corner) is held by one end of the spinnaker sheet. In hoisting, the preferred method consists of a series of actions performed in rapid succession in such a way that no one has to leave the cockpit. (Putting a man on the foredeck makes the boat easy to tip.) The division of duties among the men depends on the ability of each. The first phase, getting ready (*right*), is completed before reaching the mark that begins leeward leg. Hoisting the spinnaker in the lee of the mainsail where there is relatively little wind (*page 56*) starts as the boat rounds the mark. Then, as the spinnaker fills, the jib is dropped (*page 57*). A well-drilled crew will have spinnaker flying within 10 seconds after mark is turned.

SPINNAKER READY to hoist (*in box*) is prepared first by leading guy (1) through lead block (2) and attaching to spinnaker tack (3); second, by snapping pole fitting (4) onto guy, raising the pole with topping lift (5) and attaching pole to fitting (6) on mast; third, by leading sheet (7) through lead block (8) and attaching sheet to spinnaker clew (9); and last, by running halyard (10) outside jib and attaching halyard to head of spinnaker (11).

HOISTING SPINNAKER, halyard pulls sail up mast while sail hangs limp in lee of the mainsail. Sheet pulls the clew aft momentarily to prevent the sail from twisting. Guy is pulled through pole fit-ting to bring tack toward the end of pole.

SPINNAKER FILLING, guy has pulled tack to end of pole, drawn the pole astern, been hooked on deck and cleated. The jib is dropped onto deck as spinnaker fills. Spinnaker will set properly when sheet is eased and the lower corners made level.

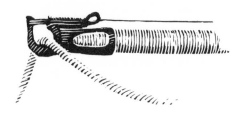

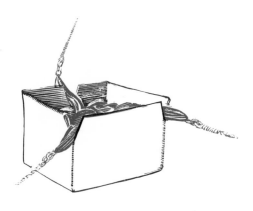

FITTINGS at each end of spinnaker pole are hooked to mast and around spin-naker guy (*above*). The guy runs freely, so sail can be raised or lowered in lee of mainsail without anyone having to go on the deck.

BOX used is heavy cardboard (carry a spare) notched with three narrow V-shaped slots. Lower corners of sail are first wedged into notches and sail is then folded into box from foot of sail up, without twisting. Head is put in last notch.

JIBING: THE MODERN, SAFE TECHNIQUE

Sailing to leeward, the skipper must always steer so that the wind (*arrow, page 60*) comes from the corner of the stern opposite the mainsail. If the skipper wishes to set a new downwind course which shifts wind to the other corner of the stern, then the position of the mainsail must be reversed (or jibed). Since the spinnaker pole must always be kept on the side opposite the mainsail, the spinnaker must be jibed simultaneously. Jibing is the most difficult and dangerous maneuver in sailing. Close attention to the method described below, which until now has been perfected only by a few expert sailors, will make safe jibing relatively easy. This method keeps all the men in the cockpit so that the stability of the boat, always precarious in jibing, will be kept at maximum throughout the maneuver. In general, the helmsman handles the mainsail, the middle crewman is responsible for keeping the spinnaker at right angles to the wind while the boat turns beneath the sail, and the forward crewman or spinnaker man is responsible for shifting the spinnaker pole (and with it the spinnaker) from one side across to the other side.

READY FOR JIBE, skipper steers with knees, pulls back on mainsheet to make room for the spinnaker man to face aft and squeeze forward of boom vang to reach the end of spinnaker pole up on mast. Middle crewman, having released guy from deck hook, holds both guy and sheet.

BEGINNING JIBE, skipper swings tiller to bear off and pulls the mainsheet rapidly in. The spinnaker man removes pole from the mast and snaps sheet into pole fitting, while the middle crewman slacks the sheet and trims guy to keep the spinnaker full and at right angles to wind.

61

HALFWAY IN JIBE, men duck as wind swings the mainsail rapidly across the cockpit. Skipper momentarily shifts tiller in the opposite direction. Spinnaker man pulls the trip line to free the left corner of spinnaker from the left end of the pole and moves the pole to the right.

COMPLETED JIBE occurs when the spinnaker man snaps left end of the pole to mast and skipper lets mainsail all the way out on port side. By then, the skipper has tiller in his left hand and takes strain of what is now the guy in his right, so middle crewman can hook guy to deck.

CARRYING A SPINNAKER
ACROSS THE WIND

The usefulness of the spinnaker is not
limited to sailing directly or almost directly with the wind (*page 60*). The spinnaker can be carried diagonally downwind (broad reaching) or at right angles
to wind (beam reaching), as at right.
Since it is more powerful than a jib, the
spinnaker is flown whenever possible in
racing. (However, carrying spinnaker
closer to the wind than about 90° causes
it to collapse.) On a reach, pull of spinnaker is sidewise and can tip boat over
if it is allowed to heel too far. Skipper
should watch for strong puffs and bear
off more downwind, so when puff reaches
boat spinnaker will be pulling more forward, the direction in which boat has
the greatest stability. Once the boat
heels too far with its spinnaker flying,
the hull develops such weather helm
that bearing off is impossible. Then sheet
must be let out quickly and spinnaker
collapsed to bring the boat back toward
even keel.

THE FUNCTION OF FITTINGS

No two skippers will agree exactly on choice and location of fittings, but no small-boat skipper questions the usefulness of the cam-action jam cleat (*circle, below*). Pulling back and down secures any line in the jaws of the cleat, and pulling backward and up frees the line. In the recommended layout for principal fittings on a Lightning, location of several useful cam cleats is indicated. Proper selection and installation of other fittings shown below is important. For strength, mainsheet blocks are held to deck with bolts, not screws. Jibsheet blocks are lightweight for correct set of jib in light weather. Spinnaker lead blocks are set far out on stern corners. Mooring fitting is set close to the mast and far from mooring chock to keep foredeck clear.

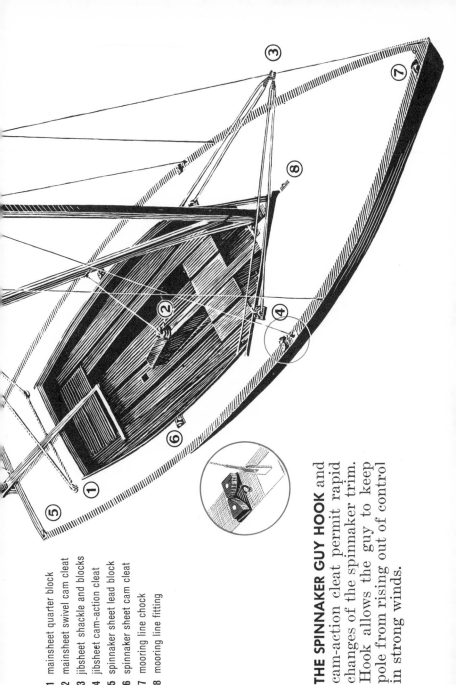

1 mainsheet quarter block
2 mainsheet swivel cam cleat
3 jibsheet shackle and blocks
4 jibsheet cam-action cleat
5 spinnaker sheet lead block
6 spinnaker sheet cam cleat
7 mooring line chock
8 mooring line fitting

THE SPINNAKER GUY HOOK and cam-action cleat permit rapid changes of the spinnaker trim. Hook allows the guy to keep pole from rising out of control in strong winds.

67

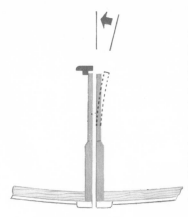

CENTERBOARD TRUNK TOP may spring sidewise with pressure, like right side of trunk shown here. This allows centerboard to wobble sideways with wave action, reduces efficiency. To prevent this, add stiffener along both top edges, as has been done (*in blue*) on the left side of trunk shown.

DESIGN OF CENTERBOARD TRUNK

Water carried inside centerboard trunk has same bad effect as that much water carried inside boat, makes hull sink lower in water. Too-wide trunk (*below, left*) is thus a handicap. Narrower trunk (*below, right*) squeezes water out of hull, makes boat float higher and reduces drag by reducing amount of hull in contact with water. Narrow slot lessens harmful tendency of centerboard to wobble, offers less frontal resistance as water hits aft end of the opening, decreases flow in and out of centerboard trunk.

BOAT FLOATS DEEPER WITH WIDE SLOT

BOAT FLOATS HIGHER WITH SLIM SLOT

THE FUNCTION OF SHAPE

As water flows past under the hull, the shapes of the chine (*page 70*) and of the three vertical underwater appendages— the centerboard, the skeg and the rudder—have an effect on speed. In the Lightning class, within the limitations of the class rules, the best results come from the use of the shapes recommended here. The over-all shape of the hull itself is rigidly controlled by a published table of permissible variations from the class blueprint. (In order to assure Lightning owners that their hull will not be outmoded, greatest hull tolerance permitted in a direction which will increase speed is only 3/8 of an inch.) Within the restrictions, the fastest hulls are those with flattest permissible run aft, narrowest beam and chines as high as permissible above water amidships.

CHINE SHAPE best for smooth flow of water past hull is a round rather than an angular shape. Rounding off corner (*in blue*) of the chine up to radius of half an inch is permitted by rules.

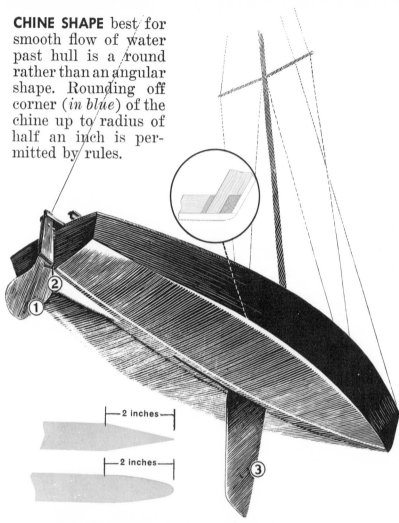

RUDDER SHAPE along lower leading edge (1 *on the hull drawing*), should be streamlined the maximum allowable two inches. Many builders make a sharp V (*diagram*), which is inefficient at all times, and especially when the rudder is turned. Correct taper has elliptical edge for a smoother flow while steering.

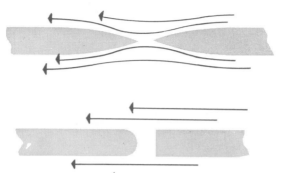

SKEG SHAPE and shape of rudder (*at 2 on hull drawing*), should create straight lines of flow. Builders who taper skeg and rudder invite water flow to bend (*blue arrows, top above*) and cause resistance. For straight lines of flow, the rudder should be as close to the skeg as possible and neither shape should be tapered (*straight arrows, above*).

CENTERBOARD SHAPE along leading edge (3 *on hull drawing opposite*), may resemble either A or B (*below*) and produce good results. (Centerboard does not cut water head on, but at about a 5° angle of leeway.) Many builders deliver boards with leading edge shaped as in C where legal one-inch taper is an angular V. This is a poor shape. Always reshape centerboard C to look like B by grinding away metal (*blue portion of* D). Legally, width of centerboard may be reduced up to ½ inch. For the trailing edge of centerboard, shape like B is best.

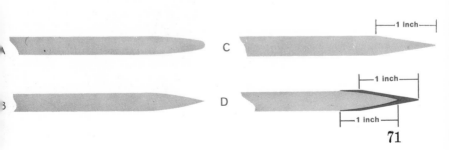

SAILING:
SPORT AT ITS BEST

*The function of sport is to renew the energy of man,
taking him away from his everyday world into another so absorbing he forgets all but the new matters
at hand. For men like Bill Cox, and for a million
others, sailing has become the answer. A sailor such
as Cox does not need high wind and lashing seas to
become intent on the action of wind and water. For
he is comfortably absorbed in making the most of
prevailing conditions in order to reach a goal—a finish line or an inlet down the shore—making the little
shifts of wind work for him. The delicate question of
the best point at which to put the tiller hard over to
come about (below) is settled and then debated in*

a. Ravielli

satisfying detail after the sail or the race is over. The process of becoming a competent sailor is not a short one, as Cox has shown, but almost every minute spent in the learning is pleasant. The first step, of course, is the purchase of a boat. The purchase of a boat has, to some extent, the same excitement that attended the purchase of a car in the early days of the auto. Its color, fittings and workmanship are all subjects of endless discussion. And many thousands of families have been buying class boats, which have established standards of construction and a live market to stabilize the price. Class boats range from 11½-foot Penguins to 70-foot 12-meter boats. (A good rule is to start small and stable and go to sleek and speedy later.) The choice of class boat may well depend on the type of fleet which is the closest. The very large class boat organizations, such as those for the Lightning and the Snipe, have fleets from coast to coast. The whereabouts of the manufacturers of class boats and the location of the closest class boat fleets can be obtained by writing Sailing Secretary, National Association of Engine and Boat Manufacturers, 420 Lexington Avenue, New York, and asking for the booklet on One-Design Sailboat Classes (available at nominal cost). Any fleet of racing sailors is always delighted to recruit new members.——THE EDITORS

4

RACING: SIGNALS, STRATEGY, STARTS

SIGNALING THE START OF A CLASS BOAT RACE

There are two types of races: match, with two boats, like the America's Cup; and fleet, with an indeterminate number of boats.

Ten minutes before the start of a race, the committee fires a gun (or blows the boat's whistle) and hoists the 10-minute warning, a white object, usually a flag or cylinder (*page 76*). Five minutes later there is another gun and a blue signal. At the start, a third gun and a red signal. If a boat starts too soon, a recall signal is given. In case of a rule violation, the innocent boat hoists a protest flag.

RACING SIGNALS

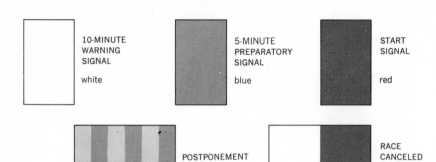

10-MINUTE WARNING SIGNAL

white

5-MINUTE PREPARATORY SIGNAL

blue

START SIGNAL

red

POSTPONEMENT

yellow and blue

RACE CANCELED FOR THE DAY

white and red

BUS MOSBACHER
ON MATCH RACING STARTS

Emil (Bus) Mosbacher, one of this country's greatest sailors, was at the helm of *Vim* in the America's Cup Trials in 1958.

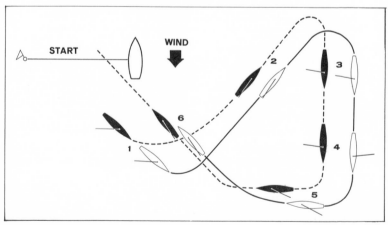

In match race start, Bus (*black*) applies
cardinal rule of always staying between
opponent and starting line. If rival
(*white*) attempts Vanderbilt start, black
stymies him by jumping on his tail as
white begins preparatory run (1) away
from line. If white tries to hold to Vanderbilt formula, black follows him to
turning point, lets white get slight overlap to windward on return run, then
leads white back to line, luffing to upset
white's timetable and ultimately crossing starting line ahead of white. If white
tries to escape by starting to tack (2),
black stays between white and line by
luffing head to wind (rules forbid white
from then completing tack). White may
then bear off sharply, but black turns inside him, coming close alongside (3) and
preventing white from jibing. Should
white by quick maneuvering manage to
complete jibe (4), black jibes inside
(5). If white at this point has sufficient
overlap to luff black, white will, accord-
ing to rules, lose luffing rights as soon as
his mast comes abeam of black's helm.
Should white then manage to slip inside
black (6), black still has advantage,
since he can once again ruin white's
timetable by luffing, or subject white to
final indignity of running him onto
wrong side of committee boat. White
must then return to line while black
races on to first mark.

Nothing is muddier to the eye of the landsman than the tactics in a sailing race, particularly a two-boat match race like the America's Cup where the competitors seem to be sailing in every direction but the right one. The diagrams below explain, in simplest general terms, a typical match race in which both boats try to follow Rule No. 1 of match racing: stay between the opponent and the next mark, no matter how far you have to go to do it.

UNDERSTANDING
A MATCH
RACE

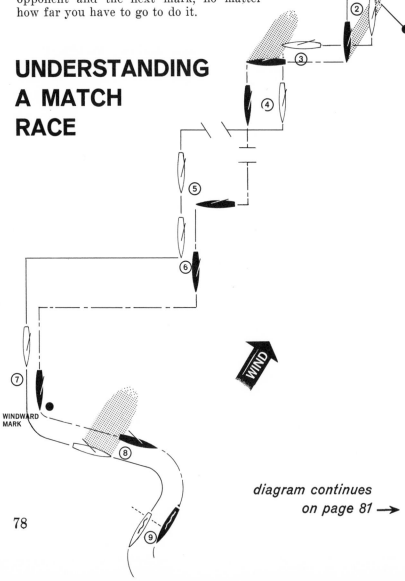

diagram continues on page 81 →

78

AT START (1), black may try to maneuver rival onto wrong side (X) of committee boat (C), forcing him to start again. Black may do this only if white is to windward. If white is to leeward, black tries to cut off white's wind, forcing white to sail in area of disturbed air, called wind shadow. But white may slip safely through to leeward (Y), thus making start even.

GOING TO WINDWARD (2), white must get away from black's wind shadow or he will be unable to pass. So he changes direction, or tacks, hoping to escape. But black immediately covers white's move (3), thus keeping white trapped by his wind shadow and at same time staying between white and the windward mark.

TACKING DUEL follows (4), with white hoping to get away by quicker maneuvering. After many tacks, white pulls even, and boats converge on opposite tacks (5). Since white is on starboard tack, *i.e.*, has wind coming over starboard side, black must give way. He tacks quickly (6) to avoid white's wind shadow.

APPROACHING THE MARK (still 6), white tacks to avoid bad wind currents bouncing off black's sail. Black comes about soon thereafter. When each skipper thinks he can lay the mark, *i.e.*, reach the mark without another tack, he comes about, heads for buoy (7).

ROUNDING THE MARK, white heads to windward (8) of black, hoping to cut off black's wind and overtake him. But black, in position of leeward boat being overtaken, has right of way, retaliates by forcing white to turn into wind until sails shake (9), and both boats lose speed. Black may continue luffing white until white's helm is opposite black's mast; then black must resume his course for the next mark.

RESUMING COURSE (10), black may be slow handling sails and white may blanket black —cut off his wind—and overtake him (11, 12). But black is not allowed to luff white again as long as some part of white's boat stays within two boat lengths sideways. However, if black can keep some part of his boat overlapping some part of white's, black may then demand room to round the buoy (13).

ROUNDING SECOND MARK (14), white is now blanketed by black. Therefore he abandons straight course for finish and, as the leeward boat, forces black to run across the wind (15), hoping black's spinnaker will collapse, so that black will slow down and white can escape. If white fails, he may then change direction by quickly jibing (16)—and black jibes to cover. By now, committee boat will have crossed to other side of starting buoy to set up finish line.

APPROACHING THE FINISH, black matches white's jibe, crossing white's stern (17) to stay on his wind. At finish, white must allow black room (18) to cross the line— unless white wants to force both boats to wrong side of buoy and gamble on winning wild scramble as boats break away from each other to circle back to finish line.

FINISH

WIND

SECOND MARK

81

Bob Mosbacher, Bus's younger brother, sailed to the North American Men's Sailing Championship in 1958, winning the Clifford D. Mallory Trophy.

BOB MOSBACHER ON FLEET RACING STARTS

If start is to leeward and first leg is short (*page 83, left*), Bob (*black boat*) favors windward end of line so he will have the inside position as he approaches the leeward mark (1) and can take the lead in rounding (2). On long leeward leg (*page 83, right*) Bob starts with wind free at leeward end of line, and then speeds up by sailing closer to wind (1) to lead rivals rounding the mark (2).

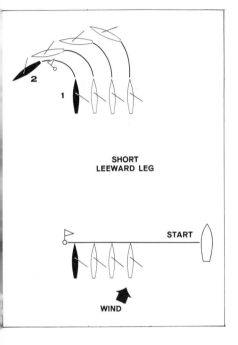

**SHORT
LEEWARD LEG**

START

WIND

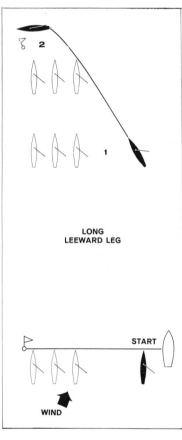

**LONG
LEEWARD LEG**

START

WIND

83

BOB MOSBACHER ON ROUNDING MARKS

GREATEST BLUNDER IS APPROACHING PORT-HAND MARK ON PORT TACK

Boat on the port tack (*black*) approaching windward mark to be left to port is sitting duck for boat on starboard tack (*white*). Rules say port tack must give way to starboard tack, so white simply holds course, forcing black to bear off and pass behind him. Black thus loses perhaps two lengths in rounding the mark.

OVERSTANDING STARBOARD-HAND MARK OPENS GATE TO PORT TACK BOAT

Black boat on port tack approaching the mark to be left to starboard has chance if he overstands or aims 1½ boat lengths above mark. White, on starboard tack, thus has room to round mark inside black, ordinarily correct move, but disastrous if black times his countermove as he should (*page 86, top*).

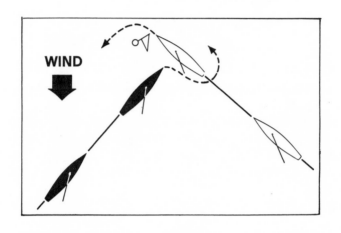

WIND

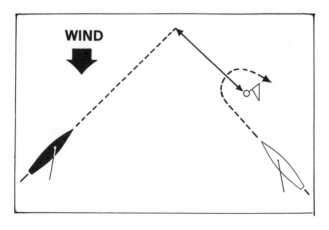

WIND

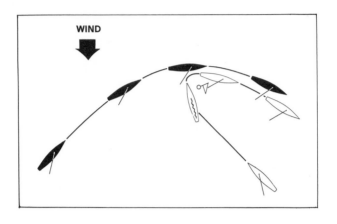

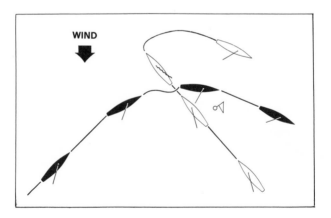

PORT TACK BOAT ROUNDS MARK WIDE, TAKES STARBOARD'S WIND

If white boat makes conventional move of rounding mark inside of black, then black can slowly bear off, leaving white just enough room to turn mark. As black bears off, he lets out sails, increasing speed, while white loses some of his speed in coming about. Once around the mark, black is sitting squarely on white's wind.

WHITE COUNTERS BY OVER SHOOT-ING BUT BLACK SLIPS INSIDE

If white anticipates black's move, white may then try to counter by over-shooting or sailing past mark, hoping to force black to go about and head away from the mark. In this case black lets white come on, then slips behind him (slowing if necessary) close to buoy and emerges several boat lengths in front, with wind clear.

ROUNDING LEEWARD MARK

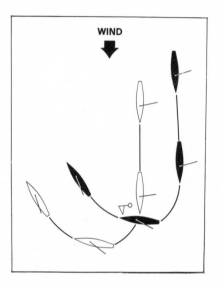

Bob Mosbacher (*black*) approaches wide of mark, then turns inside white opponent, who loses lead by starting his turn too close to the buoy. This simple maneuver, unknown or unpractised by some of best sailors, can be decisive move in race, putting black on top of white in maneuvering toward next mark, or in final dash for finish line.